Peter Bell B.Ed. (Hons)

EARTH and SPACE

Photocopiable Scientific Investigations for pupils

Published by:

"TOPICAL RESOURCES"

Copyright © 1994 Peter Bell

Printed in Great Britain for "Topical Resources", publishers of Educational Materials, P.O.Box 329, Fulwood, PRESTON, PR2 4SF (Telephone 0772 863158) by T.Snape & Company Ltd., Boltons Court, Preston, Lancashire.

Typeset by Janet Nielsen, White Cross Network, White Cross, Lancaster.

First published November 1990. Second Edition May 1994.

ISBN 1 872977 01 4

INTRODUCTION

How the book is organised
This book contains twelve photocopiable science investigations at four different levels of ability. Each investigation is four pages long and includes background information, experiments to carry out, questions to answer and problems to solve. At the back of the book can be found detailed teacher's notes and worked examples.

Worked examples
The worked examples have been included to demonstrate to the reader the type of responses the teacher might expect. However, it must be realised that Primary Science is not an exact art and a variety of responses may be taken as being correct. What is marked as correct in individual cases is a matter for the teacher's own professional judgement. The examples given SHOULD NOT be used as answer sheets.

Organising the Activities
Twelve pupil investigations of varying degrees of difficulty are included on the theme of "Earth and Space". It is envisaged that these investigations could be used to provide the Experimental Science element of a wider primary school topic on Earth and Space which may last for about half a term. It is not envisaged that every pupil will be involved in every investigation. It is more likely that small groups of 2 to 6 pupils will carry out 3 or 4 investigations and then report back their findings to the rest of the class. The teacher will play an important role in bringing together all of the information reported and drawing out the underlying scientific ideas.

Presentation of finished work
The old fashioned virtues of neatness and accuracy (which, in the author's opinion, can so easily be lost when using worksheets) may be maintained by either (i) working a 'rough' worksheet first in pencil which is corrected and then written up in ink on a second worksheet or (ii) using a 'rough book' for the original work and again writing a final report on the worksheet in ink.

Levels of ability
The author has attempted to grade the investigations in line with the statements of attainment found within the attainment targets. As this is a relatively new concept in primary science, the teacher should recognise that, although every attempt has been made to make sure the gradings are accurate, small differences of opinion may occur.

Grouping of pupils
Grading the difficulty of investigation will challenge the teacher to think carefully about grouping the children. The teacher may have groups of more able children working on the higher levels and groups of less able children working on the lower levels. Alternatively, mixed ability groups may attempt all levels of activity with the teacher observing the contributions made by individual members of the group. Many variations on this theme are possible.

Reading Age and Level 2 activities
The author recognises that less able or younger children working on Level 2 may need adult help with reading the text and organising their investigations.

The 12 Earth and Space Investigations are:

(1) WHERE DO YOU LIVE? - Level 2
(2) HOW ARE SHADOWS MADE? - Level 2
(3) HOW DO ROCKETS GET INTO SPACE? - Level 3
(4) HOW DO ROCKETS RETURN TO EARTH? - Level 3
(5) HOW CAN MESSAGES BE SENT? - Level 3
(6) DOES THE MOON CHANGE SHAPE? - Level 3
(7) WHY DO WE HAVE DAY AND NIGHT? - Level 4
(8) HOW DO ASTRONAUTS STAY ALIVE IN SPACE? - Level 4
(9) WHAT IS GRAVITY? - Level 4
(10) WHY ARE SUMMER DAYS LONGER THAN WINTER DAYS? - Level 4
(11) WHAT IS A STAR? - Level 5
(12) WHAT IS THE SOLAR SYSTEM? - Level 5

(Use this outline to design a front cover for your Topic Booklet.)

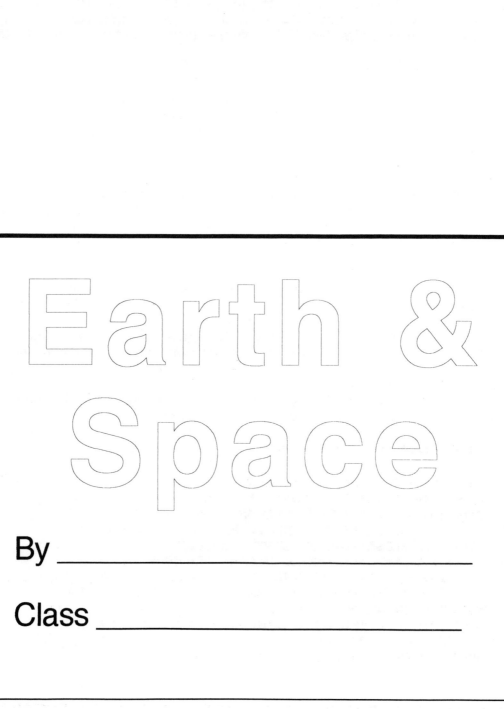

Earth & Space

By _____

Class _____

© Topical Resources. May be photocopied for classroom use only.

WHERE DO YOU LIVE?

Imagine you wake up one morning and find a glass bottomed rocket near your house. You climb inside, close the door and press some buttons.

Suddenly the engines fire and you start to take off. At first you can see your house, your road, your town but as you climb higher, things begin to look different.

Experiment 1 - Can you make a toy car seem to shrink?

Find a small toy car and place it on a desk or shelf. Take one step back and look at it carefully. Take 10 steps back and look again. Now try 20 steps. Now start your report.

Date: _____

Title: _____

Picture of what you did.

[ ]

I needed a _____

After 1 step back the car looked _____

_____

After 10 steps back the car looked _____

_____

After 20 steps back the car looked _____

_____

I think this happened because _____

_____

Experiment 2 - How do Maps and Globes appear from a distance?

Find a street map, a map of England, a globe and a small ball. Walk away from each object in turn. What do you notice? Start your report.

Date: _____

Title: _____

Picture of what you did.

I needed a _____

When I walked away from the street map I noticed _____
_____

When I walked away from the England map I noticed _____
_____

When I walked away from the globe I noticed _____
_____

A friend held the small ball next to the globe. When I walked away I noticed _____
_____

© Topical Resources. May be photocopied for classroom use only. E & S Investigation 1 Page 3

Questions to answer

1) What might you see from the window of your rocket as you climb higher and higher into a clear blue sky?

_____
_____
_____
_____

2) Write your address here.

House number or name → _____

Road, street, avenue, close etc → _____

← Town _____

County → _____

Country → _____

Planet! → _____

Problems to solve

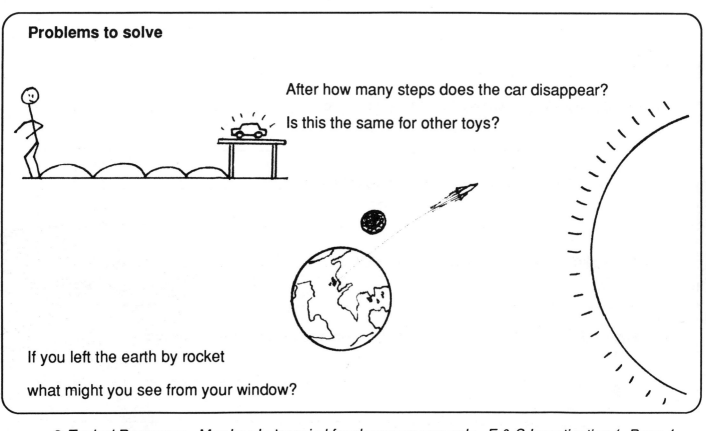

After how many steps does the car disappear?

Is this the same for other toys?

If you left the earth by rocket what might you see from your window?

HOW ARE SHADOWS MADE?

If you stand in the playground on a sunny day you will find you have a friend. She or he walks when you walk, runs when you run and skips when you skip. Every action will be copied exactly. Sometimes your shadow will be very long and at other times very short. Sometimes your shadow will be very clear. At other times you can hardly see it at all.

© Topical Resources. May be photocopied for classroom use only. E & S Investigation 2 Page 1

Experiment 1 - Can you make shadows indoors?

Stand a pencil on its end in the middle of a white sheet of paper. (Blu-tack will help). Shine a torch at the pencil to make a shadow. Try to make the shadow move. Try to make long or short shadows. Try to make shadows of other things.

EXPERIMENT REPORT

Date: _____ Title: _____

_____

Diagram

[   ]

The things I used were _____
_____

This is what I did _____
_____

I made long shadows by _____
_____

I made short shadows by _____
_____

I made the shadows move by _____
_____

I made other shadows using _____
_____

© *Topical Resources. May be photocopied for classroom use only.*

Experiment 2 - How can you tell the time using shadows?

You need a sunny day for this experiment. Find a flat piece of wood with a large nail in the middle and a compass. At 10.00 am place the board in the sun making sure the N points to North. Use chalk to mark the shadow. Do the same every hour for the rest of the day. Check and time your chalk marks another day.

EXPERIMENT REPORT

Date: _____ Title: _____
_____

Diagram

[ ]

The things I used were _____
_____

This is what I did _____
_____
_____

I made sure the board was always pointing the same way by _____
_____

I noticed that during one day the shadow _____
_____
_____

With the board pointing exactly the same way at 10.00 am, on another day I noticed that __
_____

Questions to answer

1) What might you see in a sunny playground? _____
_____

2) Do shadows always look the same? _____
_____

3) How can we make shadows inside? _____
_____

4) Do outside shadows change from morning to afternoon? _____
_____

5) How can shadows be used to tell the time? _____
_____

6) What causes shadows outside? _____
_____

Problems to solve

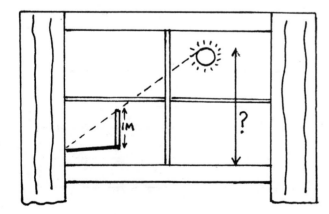

What would you notice in sunshine records (height of sun at midday - length of metre stick shadow at midday) over a period of six months.

What is a sundial?

Who used them?

When were they used?

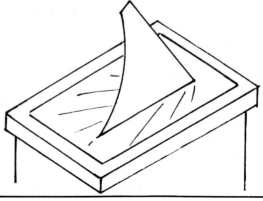

HOW DO ROCKETS GET INTO SPACE?

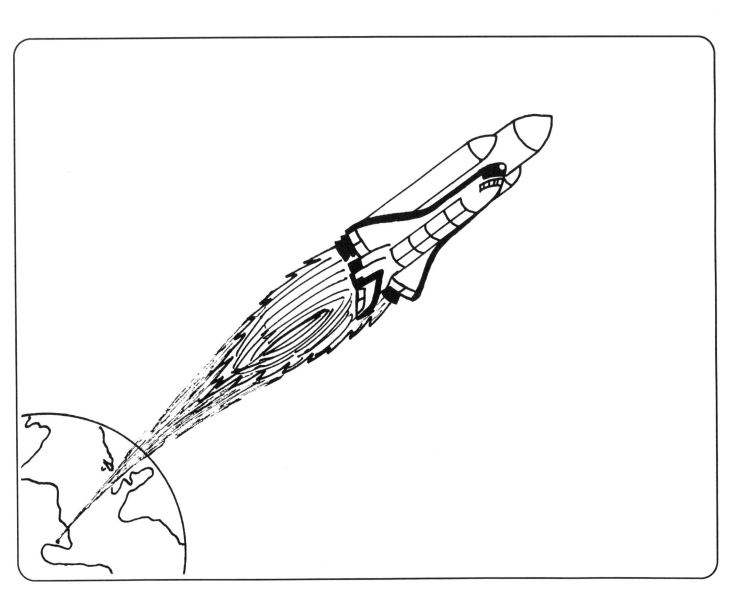

To get into space a rocket must burn its fuel. The great heat causes gases to expand (grow bigger and bigger) very quickly. The hot gases rush out of the bottom forcing the rocket to lift into the sky. In order to leave the earth, the gases must push the rocket up harder than the earth tries to pull the rocket down. The earth pulls with a force called GRAVITY.

Experiment 1 - How high can you throw a ball?

Throw a tennis ball as high as you can into the air. Estimate how high it goes. Ask two or three friends to do the same. Now ask an adult. Who threw the ball the highest? Why?

EXPERIMENT REPORT

Date: _____ Title: _____

_____

Diagram

[blank box]

The things I used were _____

_____

This is what I did. _____

_____

_____

The ball was thrown highest by _____

_____

The lowest ball was thrown by _____

_____

I think _____ threw the ball the highest because _____

_____

_____

© Topical Resources. May be photocopied for classroom use only. E & S Investigation 3 Page 2.

Experiment 2 - Can you make a classroom rocket?

Blow up a balloon and let it go. What happens? Find a cut-away washing up liquid bottle with a balloon attached. Blow up the balloon and hang your 'rocket' on to a piece of nylon line stretched across the room. Let go. What happens?

EXPERIMENT REPORT

Date: _____ Title: _____

_____

Diagram

[ ]

The things I used were _____

_____

This is what I did. _____

_____

_____

The first balloon went _____

_____

The balloon fastened to the line went _____

_____

The greatest distance we flew the line balloon was _____

_____

Questions to answer

1) What does the rocket burn? _____
   _____

2) What does the fuel turn into? _____
   _____

3) What pushes the rocket up? _____
   _____

4) What brought the ball back to earth? _____
   _____

5) What must the rocket overcome to leave the earth? _____
   _____

6) What made the balloon move? _____
   _____

Problems to solve

How high can you throw a ball? Try different sizes and balls made of different materials.

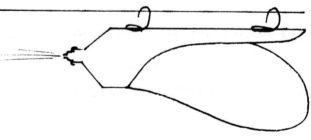

How far can you fire your rocket along the nylon line? Try different sizes and shapes of balloon.

© *Topical Resources. May be photocopied for classroom use only.* E & S Investigation 3 Page 4.

HOW DO ROCKETS RETURN TO EARTH?

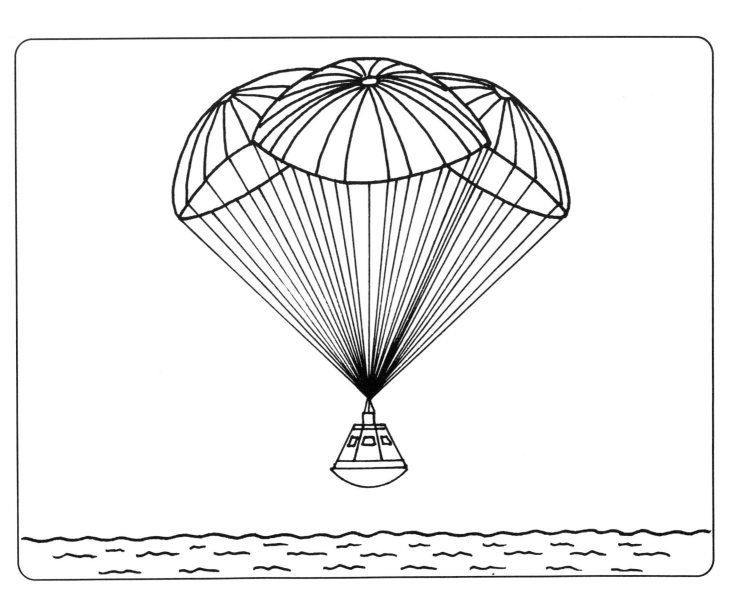

The Space Shuttle is a re-usable spacecraft. This means it can fly back to earth and be used again. Before the Shuttle was built, all spacecraft landed using parachutes. A large rocket would carry men in a small capsule into space. When all the fuel was used up, the rocket was left in space and only the capsule with the astronauts inside returned to Earth. The capsule was lowered gently to Earth by parachutes.

Experiment 1 - How quickly do things drop?

Take two sheets of paper the same size and screw one into a ball. Stand on a chair and let them go at the same time. Which hits the ground first? Why? Try different shaped pieces of paper.

EXPERIMENT REPORT

Date: _____ Title: _____

_____

Diagram

The things I used were _____

_____

This is what I did. _____

_____

_____

The piece of paper which hit the ground first was _____

_____

_____

I think this happened because _____

_____

_____

Experiment 2 - Can you make a toy parachute?

Cut a large square of very thin 'plastic bag material', sellotape a length of cotton to each corner and tie the ends to a clothes peg. Throw it into the air and observe what happens. Improve your design.

EXPERIMENT REPORT

Date: _____ Title: _____

_____

Diagram

```
┌─────────────────────────────────────────────────┐
│                                                 │
│                                                 │
│                                                 │
│                                                 │
│                                                 │
│                                                 │
└─────────────────────────────────────────────────┘
```

The things I used were _____

_____

This is what I did. _____

_____

_____

When I threw the parachute in the air _____

_____

_____

I tried to improve my parachute by _____

_____

_____

Questions to answer

1) What is special about the Space Shuttle? _____
_____

2) How did the spacecraft land before the shuttle? _____
_____

3) What used to be left in space? _____
_____

4) Who travelled inside the space capsule? _____
_____

5) Why did one sheet of paper fall slowly? _____
_____

6) How does the space shuttle return to earth? _____
_____

Problems to solve

Does using different materials for the sail alter the performance of your parachute?

Can you improve your parachute by changing its shape, the number of strings, the weight it carries etc?

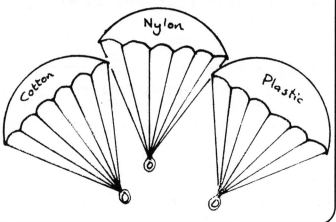

HOW CAN MESSAGES BE SENT?

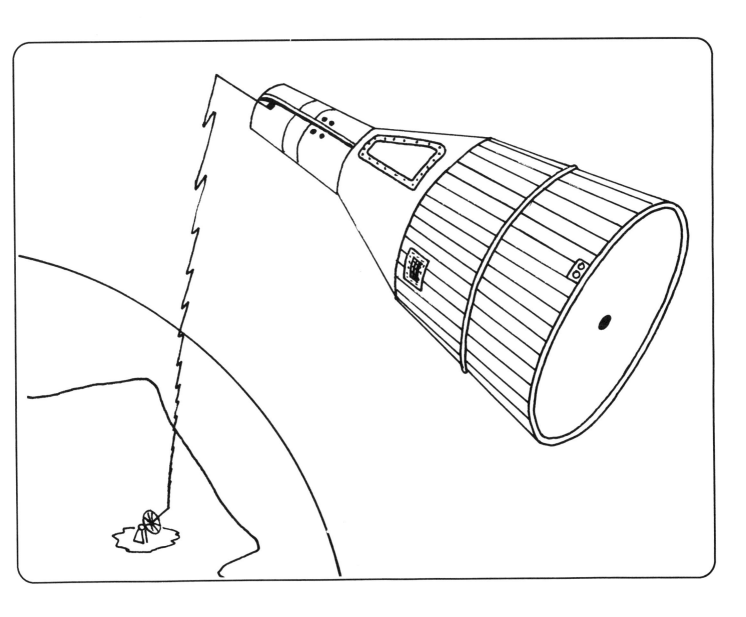

When a rocket or space shuttle is sent into orbit the astronauts need to talk to base. They use T.V. and radio to do this. A camera in the spacecraft takes pictures. A transmitter sends electrical signals to earth. A receiving aerial collects the signals and sends them to a television on the ground. No wires are needed to connect the spacecraft to base control.

Experiment 1 - Can you make a washing-up liquid bottle telephone?

Find two washing-up liquid bottles which have been cut in half. Connect some plastic tubing to the nozzles. Can this be used as a simple telephone? Will it work round corners?

EXPERIMENT REPORT

Date: _____ Title: _____

_____

Diagram

The things I used were _____
_____

This is what I did. _____
_____
_____

When I spoke into the washing-up liquid bottle _____
_____
_____

When we tried our 'telephone' round a corner _____
_____
_____

© Topical Resources. May be photocopied for classroom use only. E & S Investigation 5 Page 2.

Experiment 2 - Can you send sound along a string?

Find or make a string telephone using two tins and a piece of string. Pull the string tight and try to speak to your partner. What happens? Will it work if the string is slack? Will it work round corners?

EXPERIMENT REPORT

Date: _____ Title: _____

_____

Diagram

The things I used were _____
_____

This is what I did. _____
_____
_____

When I tried to speak to my partner _____
_____

When the string was slack _____
_____

We tried it round a corner and _____
_____

Questions to answer

1) How do astronauts speak to earth? _____
   _____

2) What does the camera in the spacecraft do? _____
   _____

3) What does the transmitter do? _____
   _____

4) What does the receiving aerial do? _____
   _____

5) Is the spacecraft connected to base control by wires? _____
   _____

6) Why do you think it is important to have a tight string on your telephone? _____
   _____

Problems to solve

What is the greatest distance your string telephone will work over? Can you improve the design? Can you make a speaking <u>and</u> a listening part?

Research other ways of sending messages.

How did the Romans send messages?

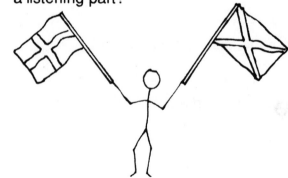

DOES THE MOON CHANGE SHAPE?

The earth goes round the sun. At the same time, the moon goes round the earth.

The biggest thing you can see in the night sky is the moon, but it is not really as big and bright as it looks. The moon only looks big to us because it is relatively close. The sun and stars are much larger but look smaller than the moon because they are much further away.

The moon is like a huge piece of rock or a small planet which orbits the earth. It is the earth's only natural satellite. It is approx. 384,000 km from Earth and is about 1/4 of the Earth's diameter. The gravity on the moon is only about 1/6 of the earths. This means you could jump 6 times as high as you could on the earth.

The moon shines by reflected light. Sunlight falls on the moon's surface and is reflected from it to earth. If you watch the moon week by week, it appears to change shape.

Experiment 1 - Why can you not see the back of the Moon?

Choose one person to be the 'earth' and another to be the 'moon'. Ask the 'moon' to walk round the earth in a circle without showing his back - the earth turning on the spot to face the moon. Can it be done?

EXPERIMENT REPORT

Date: _____ Title: _____

_____

Diagram

Equipment needed: _____

_____

_____

Method used: _____

_____

_____

Observations made: _____

_____

_____

Why do you think we cannot see the back of the Moon from the Earth's surface? _____

_____

_____

Experiment 2 - Does the Moon change shape?

Use a lamp to represent the sun and a small white ball to represent the Moon in a darkened room. Stand about 1 m from the lamp. (You represent the earth). Move the white ball round your head. What shadow shapes do you observe on the white ball?

EXPERIMENT REPORT

Date: _____ Title: _____

_____

Diagram

Equipment needed: _____

_____

_____

Method used: _____

_____

_____

_____

Observations made: _____

_____

_____

Why do you think the moon appears to change shape week by week? _____

_____

_____

Questions to answer

1) Why does the moon look so large in the night sky? _____
_____

2) Is the moon larger than the sun? _____
_____

3) What is an unnatural satellite? _____
_____

4) How many people do you think you could lift if you were standing on the moon? _____
_____

5) What makes the moon 'light up'? _____
_____

6) Does the moon change its shape? _____
_____

Problems to solve

Can you make accurate observations of the Moon's surface using binoculars or a telescope?

Devise and carry out a way of recording Moon observations over a period of one month.

WHY DO WE HAVE DAY AND NIGHT?

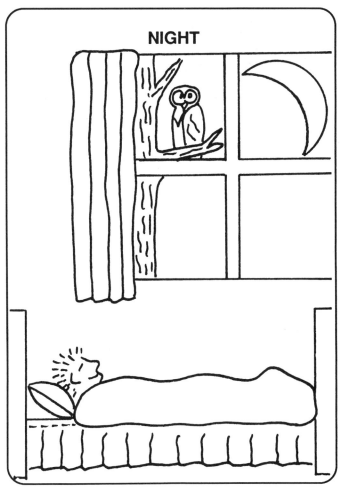

Each day we get up in the morning and go to school or do other things. Towards the end of the day we may have supper and go to bed. We have day and night. In summer it is light when we wake up and light when we go to bed. In winter it is dark when we get up and dark when we go to bed.

In summer day is longer than night.   In winter night is longer than day.

Experiment 1 - How can you make light and dark?

Find a closed box with a small hole to peep through and a larger hole for a torch. Put a toy car inside the box. Now start your report.

Date: _____

Title: _____

Picture of what you did.

I needed a _____

_____

I peeped inside with the torch switched on and I could see _____

_____

With the torch switched off I could see _____

_____

To make daylight inside the box I needed _____

_____

_____

Experiment 2 - How can you make day and night?

Find a globe and a torch. Shine the torch onto the globe. (The torch is like the sun. The globe is like the earth). Put a small piece of blu-tack on England. Turn the globe slowly anticlockwise. Start your report.

Date: _____

Title: _____

Picture of what you did.

I needed a _____

I shone the torch onto _____
_____

England was in day light when _____
_____

England was in darkness when _____
_____

The globe turning round in front of a light and then away from the light makes us have ___
_____

Questions to answer

1) What do we do in the morning? _____

2) What do we do at night time? _____

3) When do we get our longest days? _____

4) When do we get our longest nights? _____

5) What do we need for day light? _____

6) Why do we have day and night? _____

Problems to solve

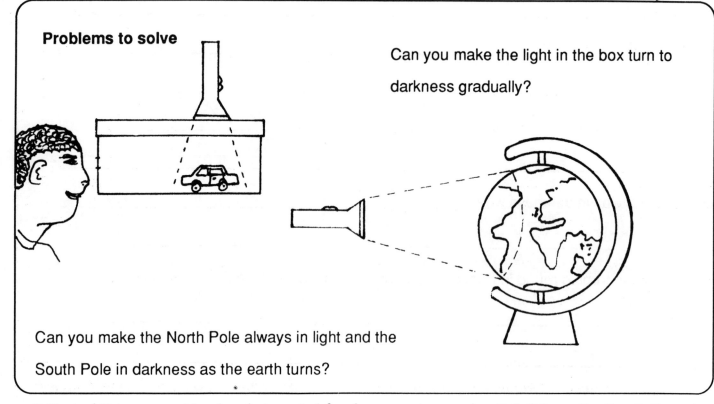

Can you make the light in the box turn to darkness gradually?

Can you make the North Pole always in light and the South Pole in darkness as the earth turns?

© Topical Resources. May be photocopied for classroom use only. E & S Investigation 7 Page 4.

HOW DO ASTRONAUTS STAY ALIVE IN SPACE?

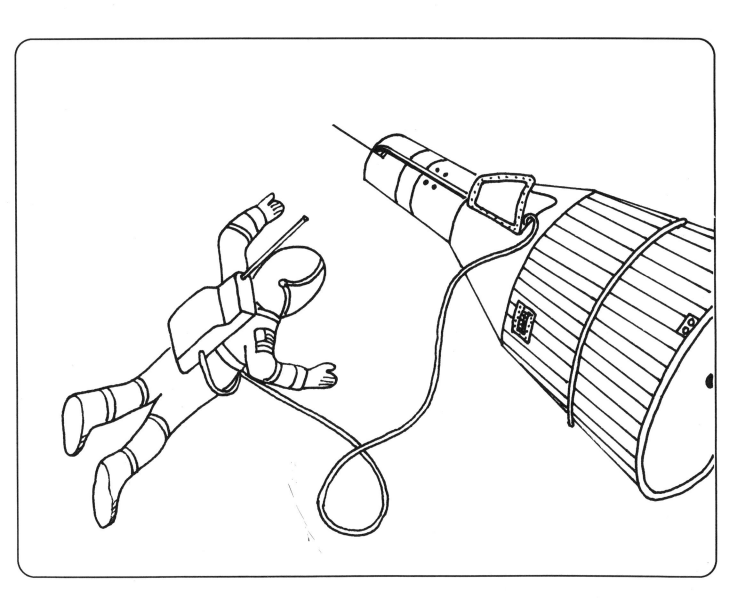

Astronauts do not wear special space suits when they are inside their spacecraft, but sometimes they have to go outside to carry out repairs or set up experiments. The space suits are connected to the spacecraft by long cables. The suits have air tanks so the astronaut can breathe. They also have to keep the astronaut at the right temperature. In space or on the moon it is hotter than an oven in the sun's light, but cooler than a freezer in the shade.

Experiment 1 - How can we keep things warm?

You will need two empty 'coke tins, a cardboard box with a lid, a thermometer, some torn up newspaper and some very hot water. Put one tin in the box and pack round with newspaper scraps. Fill the tins with hot water. Use a thermometer to measure how hot the water is every five minutes.

EXPERIMENT REPORT

Date: _____ Title: _____

_____

Diagram

Equipment needed: _____

Method used: _____

Observations made:

TIME	Temperature of tin in air	Temperature of tin in box
0 minutes	°C	°C
5 minutes	°C	°C
10 minutes	°C	°C
15 minutes	°C	°C
20 minutes	°C	°C
25 minutes	°C	°C
30 minutes	°C	°C

Which tin stayed warm the longer? Why? _____

Experiment 2 - How can we keep things cool?

You will need two empty 'coke tins, thermometer and a plastic margarine tub. Fill the tins with hot water. Put one tin into the margarine tub. Place the margarine tub under a running cold tap. Use a thermometer to measure how hot the water is in each can, every five minutes.

EXPERIMENT REPORT

Date: _____ Title: _____
_____

Diagram

Equipment needed: _____
_____

Method used: _____
_____
_____

Observations made:

TIME	Temperature of tin in air	Temperature of tin in tub
0 minutes	°C	°C
5 minutes	°C	°C
10 minutes	°C	°C
15 minutes	°C	°C
20 minutes	°C	°C
25 minutes	°C	°C
30 minutes	°C	°C

Which tin cooled more quickly? _____
_____

Questions to answer

1) Why do you think astronauts don't need to wear their space suits inside the spacecraft?
_____
_____

2) Why do the suits have air tanks?_____
_____

3) How could a space suit be made to cool an astronaut down? _____
_____

4) What could be done to make sure a space suit stayed nice and warm?_____
_____

5) Why is the astronaut fastened to the spacecraft by a cable? _____
_____

6) Do you think a space suit would be comfortable to wear ? Why?_____
_____

Problems to solve

How good are other materials at keeping water warm?

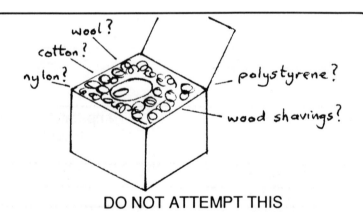

DO NOT ATTEMPT THIS WITHOUT AN ADULT'S HELP.

How quickly can you make boiling water in a coke can go cold?

WHAT IS GRAVITY?

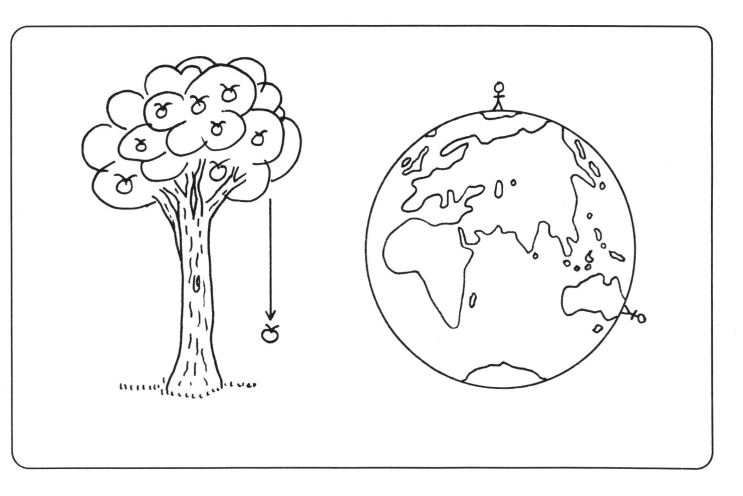

What makes an apple fall out of a tree and hit the ground? Why do people in Australia not fall off the earth and end up floating around in space? The answer to both of these questions is "gravity". The earth has an invisible pull or force which attracts everything in much the same way as a magnet attracts some metal objects. This invisible force pulls everything towards the centre of the earth, that is why objects we drop fall downwards to land on the ground. In space there is no gravity. Astronauts can push themselves in any direction and they will continue moving in that direction until they eventually touch something solid.

Experiment 1 - Do heavy objects fall more quickly?

Hold a stone in your hand. Let it go. What happens? Hold a large stone and a small stone at the same height. Let them go at exactly the same time. Which landed first? Was your test fair?

EXPERIMENT REPORT

Date: _____ Title: _____

_____

Diagram

Equipment needed: _____

_____

_____

Method used: _____

_____

_____

Observations made: _____

_____

_____

Do heavy objects fall more quickly than light ones? _____

_____

_____

Experiment 2 - Does gravity work on a slope?

Ask your teacher for a washing-up liquid aeroplane. Thread some nylon line through the nozzles of the plane. Hold one end of the line high and one end low. Let go of the plane. What happens? When does it move most quickly?

EXPERIMENT REPORT

Date: _____ Title: _____

_____

Diagram

Equipment needed: _____
_____
_____

Method used _____
_____
_____

Observations made: _____
_____
_____

What made the plane move along the line? _____
_____
_____

Questions to answer

1) What makes an apple fall out of a tree? _____
_____

2) What do magnets attract? _____
_____

3) What does gravity attract? _____
_____

4) What happens to astronauts in space? _____
_____

5) Which way did the stones always fall? Why? _____
_____

6) What made the model plane slide down the string? _____
_____

Problems to solve

Can you make a machine that will drop two different stones at exactly the same time?

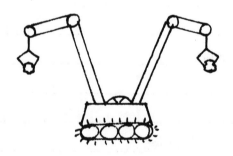

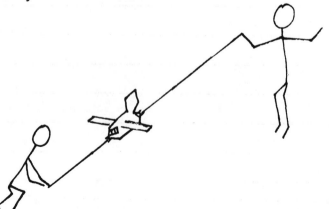

Can you make a nylon line plane which will travel faster than any other?

WHY ARE SUMMER DAYS LONGER THAN WINTER DAYS?

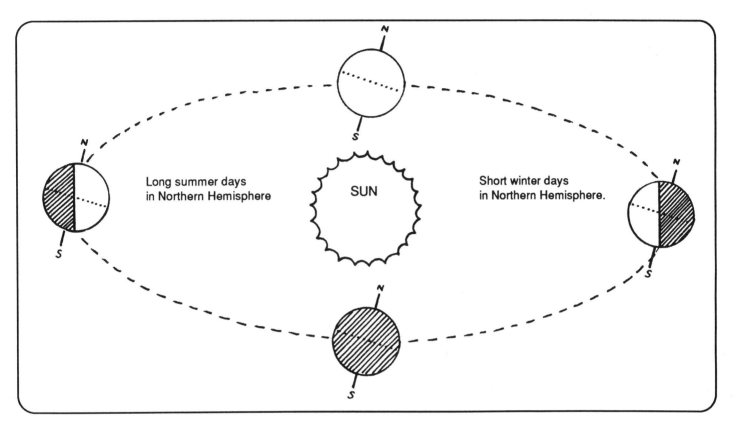

The earth turns on its own axis once every 24 hours. For part of that time you will face the sun and be in daylight. For the rest of the time you will be away from the sun and hence be in darkness. This gives us day and night.

At the same time, the earth moves round the sun. The time taken for the earth to make one complete journey around the sun is one year.

The axis of the earth (if you like, an imaginary axil which the earth spins round) is tilted in space at a slight angle. This means, at one end of the year, the Northern Hemisphere receives more sunlight than the Southern Hemisphere, hence the North gets long summer days. At the other end of the year the Southern Hemisphere receives most sunlight - the Northern Hemisphere then gets short winter days.

The tilt of the earth also causes summer days to be hotter than winter days. Changes of temperature and length of day cause seasonal changes.

Experiment 1 - Why are days longer in summer and shorter in winter?

You need a table lamp without a shade (sun) and a white ball (earth) with N & S hemispheres marked and a knitting needle pushed through from N to S. Work in a darkened room. Hold the knitting needle at a slight angle pointing towards a corner of the room. Move the earth round the sun keeping the needle pointing towards the same corner. Turn the ball to represent day and night. Observe the shadow made on the ball.

EXPERIMENT REPORT

Date: _____ Title: _____

_____

Diagram

Equipment needed: _____

_____

_____

Method used: _____

_____

_____

Observations made: _____

_____

_____

At what position does the Northern Hemisphere have its longest days? _____

_____

At what position does the Northern Hemisphere have its shortest days? _____

_____

Experiment 2 - Why is is hotter in summer than in winter?

Shine a torch directly onto a flat piece of squared paper. Draw round the spot of light. Now tilt the paper keeping it the same distance from the torch at the centre of the spot. Observe what happens to the shape at the spot of light. Draw round the new shape. Measure the area of both shapes.

EXPERIMENT REPORT

Date: _____ Title: _____

_____

Diagram

Equipment needed: _____

_____

Method used: _____

_____

Observations made: _____

_____

The same amount of light comes from the torch each time. In which shape is the light most spread out? _____

_____

Under a very strong light the paper would heat up. Which shape would be hottest? _____

_____

Why is it hotter in summer than winter? _____

_____

Questions to answer

1) Why do we have day and night? _____
_____

2) How long does it take the earth to make one orbit of the sun? _____
_____

3) Why are days longer in summer? _____
_____

4) How many seasons do we have in one year? _____
_____

5) What are the causes of seasonal changes? _____
_____

6) How does the earth's inclination to the sun change from summer to winter? _____
_____

Problems to solve

Heat comes from the sun in the same way as light. Prove that heat rays are most concentrated on the British Isles in the summer.

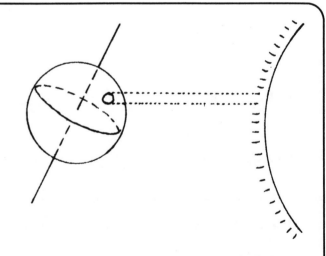

Research the seasons experienced by the North Pole and the Equator.

WHAT IS A STAR?

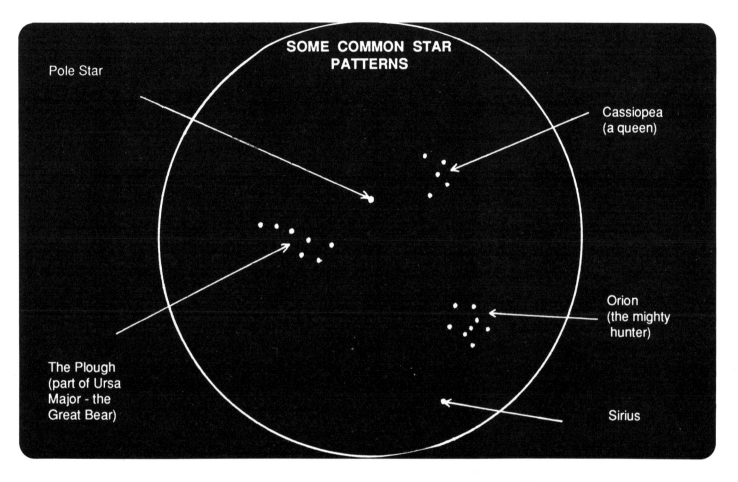

The sun is a star with a family of planets going round it. This family is called our solar system. The sun itself is made of a seething mass of white hot gases. Even though it is over 100 times wider than the Earth, it is only a small star. Some stars are over 500 times larger than our sun. One of the nearest stars to us is call Sirius, the Dog Star. It is a bright star which can be seen low down on the Southern horizon in the winter months.

If you look closely at the night sky you will see groups of stars which make patterns. These patterns are called constellations and over the years have been given names such as The Plough, Cassiopea and Orion.

Experiment 1 - Can you make a working model telescope?

You need two tubes about 20cm long. One tube should fit inside the other. You also need blu-tack and two lenses (ask your teacher). Use blu-tack to fit a lens into one end of each tube. Fit the tubes together. Use your telescope to make observations in and around your classroom.
* NEVER LOOK DIRECTLY AT THE SUN*

EXPERIMENT REPORT

Date: _____ Title: _____

_____

Diagram

Equipment needed _____
_____

Method used. _____
_____
_____

Observations made. _____
_____
_____

Did moving the two tubes effect how clearly you could see through the telescope? _____
_____
_____

Experiment 2 - Do stars move across our night sky?

Copy the front page diagram onto a 1m circle of sugar paper. Pin this to the ceiling in the centre of your classrooom. Stand in a corner of the room and with your telescope observe the star patterns. Keeping watch, walk slowly anti-clockwise round the classroom. What do you notice?

EXPERIMENT REPORT

Date: _____ Title: _____

_____

Diagram

Equipment needed _____

_____

_____

Method used. _____

_____

_____

Observations made. _____

_____

_____

Did the star shapes appear to move? Why is this? _____

_____

_____

Questions to answer

1) What is another name for our sun? _____

2) What are stars made of? _____

3) Are stars larger than planets? _____

4) What is a constellation? _____

5) What tool do scientists use for studying stars? _____

6) Do stars move across our sky at night? _____

Problems to solve

Research some names of constellations.

Where did these names originate?

Dove

Use your telescope to observe the moon daily for one month. What do you notice?

WHAT IS THE SOLAR SYSTEM?

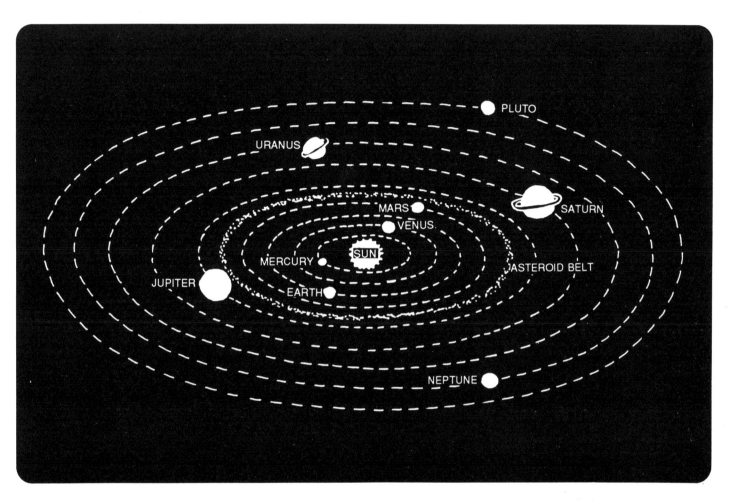

The solar system consists of the sun and everything which moves round the sun. This includes the nine major planets and their satellites. The planets orbit the sun which is one of many stars made of glowing gases. A satellite is any object which orbits a planet. The earth's only natural satellite is called the moon.

Nine planets orbit our sun. They are Mercury, Venus, Earth, Mars, Jupiter, Saturn, Uranus, Neptune and Pluto. Mercury is the planet nearest to the sun, Pluto is furthest away. Mercury is the smallest planet. Venus is similar in size to the earth. Neptune, Saturn, Jupiter and Uranus are larger than the earth. Other objects found in the solar system are asteroids, comets and meteors.

© *Topical Resources. May be photocopied for classroom use only. E & S Investigation 12 Page 1.*

Experiment 1 - Which planet takes the longest to orbit the sun?

You need 9 planet name cards and a chair. Place the chair in the middle of your playground (this represents the sun). Ask 9 pupils to hold a card and stand in planet order from the chair (sun). Walking at the same speed, ask the pupils to walk in a circle round the chair. Which pupil takes the longest?

EXPERIMENT REPORT

Date: _____   Title: _____

Diagram

Equipment needed _____

Method used. _____

Observations made. _____

Which planet do you think would take the longest to orbit the sun? _____

HOW TO MAKE A MODEL SOLAR SYSTEM

1) Use P.E. hoops to make a 1 metre diameter globe framework. Cover the frame with strips of thick paper and then papier-mache. Finally cover with yellow tissue paper. This represents the sun.

2) Make 9 planets from plasticine balls to these sizes:

   Cover the balls with papier-mache.
   Research planet colours and paint
   the models appropriately.
   Make Saturn and Uranus cardboard
   rings.

   | Mercury 1/2 cm across |
   | Venus 1 cm across |
   | Earth 1 cm across |
   | Mars 1/2 cm across |
   | Jupiter 11 cm across |
   | Saturn 9 1/2 cm across |
   | Uranus 4 cm across |
   | Neptune 4 cm across |
   | Pluto 1/4 cm across |

3) Hang the 'sun' in one corner of the classroom from the ceiling. Working diagonally across the room, use thread to suspend the planets at the following distances from the sun.

   Mercury 10 cm, Venus 20 cm, Earth 30 cm, Mars 40 cm, Jupiter 150 cm, Saturn 280 cm, Uranus 580 cm, Neptune 900 cm, Pluto 1180 cm.

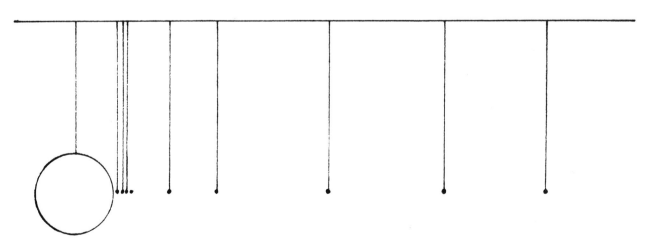

Questions to answer

1) What is the Solar System? _____
_____

2) What is a Satellite? _____
_____

3) What is the nearest planet to the sun? _____
_____

4) Which planet is furthest from the sun? _____
_____

5) Which planet orbits the sun in the shortest time? _____
_____

6) Why is this? _____
_____

Problems to solve

Space distances are enormous. For a more accurate model, times all distances from the sun by 400. Will the model fit your school field?

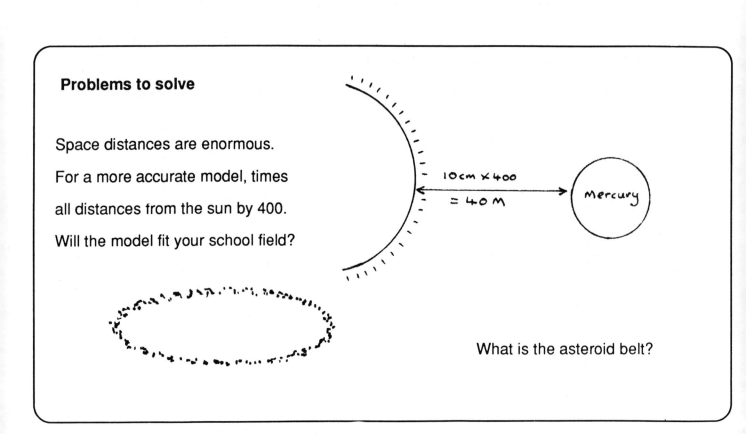

What is the asteroid belt?

Level 2 - WHERE DO YOU LIVE? - Teacher's Notes

Equipment needed: Toy car (matchbox size) - a street map of a town - open and pinned to a wall - a map of England, preferably one with counties on it to link with address (e.g. 5 Damside Street, Kendal, Cumbria) a globe - a small ball approx 1/6 size globe - it may help if it is painted grey with moon type markings - it could be labelled the moon.

Experiment 1: Aim - to help children understand that objects look smaller from a distance and that the object itself does not actually change its size.

The object should be placed in a clear position. Ideally a corridor or hall/playground should be available to be able to pace out the required distances.

A variety of responses could be made to any of the questions asked of the children. The point to be drawn out is that objects "look" smaller at a distance but do not actually change size.

Experiment 2: Aim - to help the children to understand how their picture of the earth would change as they travel further away from the earth's surface in their imaginary space rocket.

Again the objects should be placed in a clear position - the maps could be opened and pinned to a wall. Much discussion should take place as children walk away from the street map/county map/globe etc - concerning the changes they can see happening. The teacher will need to talk about the idea that the moon is like a small ball, going around the earth and demonstrate with the appropriate objects. It may be suggested that a classroom ceiling light may represent the sun shining down.

The written responses should indicate that, for example, streets can be seen clearly at first but soon merge to form one shape which becomes the town/city etc. The G.B. County shape soon becomes one land mass amongst others interspersed by seas.

Questions to answer

In writing their address, it should be pointed out that they do not just belong to one town or county but also to a wider community called the Earth.

Problems to solve

This extension activity is for those children who would like to explore the first experiment further. The second activity could be carried out in an imaginary way or by researching in picture reference books. The finished product is entirely up to the teacher and/or pupil.

Experiment 1 - Can you make a toy car seem to shrink?

Find a small toy car and place it on a desk or shelf. Take one step back and look at it carefully. Take 10 steps back and look again. Now try 20 steps. Now start your report.

Date: _Monday 15th October_
Title: _How toy cars look when you walk away from them._
Picture of what you did.

I needed a _small toy car_
After 1 step back the car looked _just the same._
After 10 steps back the car looked _as if it were smaller than before._
After 20 steps back the car looked _a lot smaller than it had been at first._
I think this happened because _when you walk away from things they look smaller than when you are close up._

Experiment 2 - How do Maps and Globes appear from a distance?

Find a street map, a map of England, a globe and a small ball. Walk away from each object in turn. What do you notice? Start your report.

Date: _Tuesday 16th October_
Title: _How maps look when you walk away from them._
Picture of what you did.

I needed _some maps, a globe and a small ball._
When I walked away from the street map I noticed _the streets seemed to look smaller and get closer together._
When I walked away from the England map I noticed _I couldn't see the towns easily but I could see the shape of Great Britain._
When I walked away from the globe I noticed _it seemed to get smaller. All I could see was land and sea._
A friend held the small ball next to the globe. When I walked away I noticed _everything seemed small. The moon was in the sky next to the earth._

Questions to answer

1) What might you see from the window of your rocket as you climb higher and higher into a clear blue sky?

From the rocket window I would see cars and houses. The streets would look smaller. I would see Great Britain and then other countries and the sea. I would see the moon next to the earth.

2) Write your address here.

House number or name → _23_   _Parklands Avenue,_ ← Road, street, avenue, close etc
Preston, ← Town
County → _Lancashire,_
Country → _England,_
Planet! → _The Earth._

Problems to solve

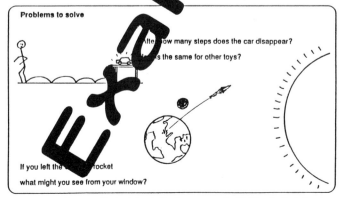

After how many steps does the car disappear? Is the same for other toys?

If you left the rocket what might you see from your window?

Level 2 - HOW ARE SHADOWS MADE? - Teacher's Notes

Equipment needed: Pencil, blu-tack or plasticine, A4 size white paper, torch, a compass, a square piece of wood approx 30 cm x 30 cm with a 10/12 cm nail driven into the middle. One side of the board should be marked north.

Experiment 1: Aim - to help children understand how shadows are made and that their length and direction can be varied.
The length of the shadows can be varied by altering the angle the light source is held at.
The direction of the shadows can be varied by altering the direction the light source shines on the object.
Different objects create different shapes of shadows. Children may like to try toy soldiers, model cars etc. Opaque objects can create interesting effects.
More distinct shadows may be created with a stronger light source such as a desk lamp.
Note: The term "diagram" is introduced here. It may be necessary to talk about its meaning.

Experiment 2: Aim - to help children understand that natural shadows change direction over the course of our day and consequently can be used for estimating the time of day.
This experiment can only be carried out on a sunny day and needs time spending on it at hourly intervals over the course of 1 or 2 days.
Children may need to be taught how to find N using a direction compass first, to enable them to place the sundial in the correct position each hour. It is important to return the board to exactly the same position each time - chalk marks may help to do this.

During the course of one day, the shadow will move round the nail. This should be consistent, and if marks are made accurately at hourly intervals, a simple sun clock will have been made.
The shadow at 10.00 am one day (providing the board is pointing in exactly the same direction) will be the same on another day.

Questions to answer

Shadows can be formed inside and outside providing a suitable light source is available. The sun is the natural source of light. Artificial light sources may be used inside.

Problems to solve

Sunshine records over six months would show that:
i) the height of the sun in the sky varies with the seasons.
ii) the length of a shadow would also vary with the time of year.

This is caused by the tilt in the earth's axis towards the sun over the course of a year.

Children may use secondary sources to research about sundials.

Experiment 1 - Can you make shadows indoors?
Stand a pencil on its end in the middle of a white sheet of paper. (Blu-tack will help). Shine a torch at the pencil to make a shadow. Try to make the shadow move. Try to make long or short shadows. Try to make shadows of other things.

Experiment 2 - How can you tell the time using shadows?
You need a sunny day for this experiment. Find a flat piece of wood with a large nail in the middle and a compass. At 10.00 am place the board in the sun making sure the N points to North. Use chalk to mark the shadow. Do the same every hour for the rest of the day. Check and time your chalk marks another day.

Problems to solve

What would you notice in sunshine records (height of sun at midday - length of metre stick shadow at midday) over a period of six months.

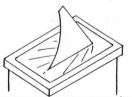

Level 3 - HOW DO ROCKETS GET INTO SPACE? - Teacher's Notes

Equipment needed: Tennis ball, various sizes and shapes of balloons, washing-up liquid bottle, nylon fishing line, two large paper clips, sellotape.

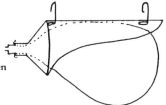

The classroom rocket is made by cutting the washing-up liquid bottle into this shape. Paper clips bent at 90° are sellotaped to the top for easy attachment to the nylon line. The balloon is held in place by pushing the open end of the balloon into the bottle opening and securing it in place with the removable nozzle from the washing-up liquid bottle.

Experiment 1: Aim - to help children understand that an object thrown into the air always returns to earth. Using people of various size and strength will ensure the ball is thrown to different heights.

The point to be drawn out is that the ball thrown with greatest force will reach the greatest height. Also, the term gravity needs to be introduced.

Experiment 2: Aim - to help the children understand that gases released very quickly can be used as a source of propulsion.

A nylon line needs to be strung across the classroom as taut as possible (if above head-height, this can be left up for the duration of the topic). For the experiment to work successfully, the paper clips must slip easily along this line. Experimenting with the size of nozzle on the washing-up liquid bottle will produce different effects and should be tested before the children attempt this experiment.

The point to be drawn out is that the sudden rush of air causes the rocket to move.

Questions to answer

The questions bring out the point that in order to leave the earth and go into orbit, a spacecraft must overcome the force of gravity.

Problems to solve

These extension activities can be attempted if time allows.

Experiment 1 - How high can you throw a ball?

Throw a tennis ball as high as you can into the air. Estimate how high it goes. Ask two or three friends to do the same. Now ask an adult. Who threw the ball the highest? Why?

Experiment 2 - Can you make a classroom rocket?

Blow up a balloon and let it go. What happens? Find a cut-away washing up liquid bottle with a balloon attached. Blow up the balloon and hang your 'rocket' on to a piece of nylon line stretched across the room. Let go. What happens?

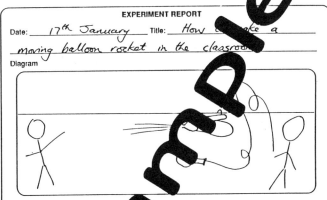

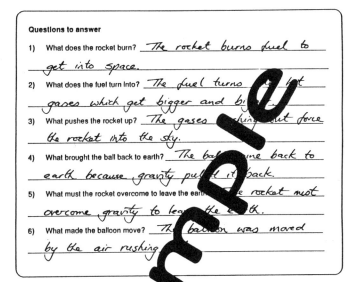

Problems to solve

How high can you throw a ball? Try different sizes and balls made of different materials.

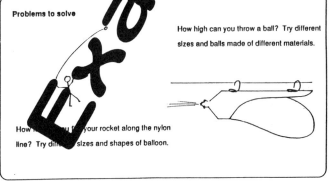

How far can you fly your rocket along the nylon line? Try different sizes and shapes of balloon.

Level 3 - HOW DO ROCKETS RETURN TO EARTH? - Teacher's Notes

Equipment needed: Several sheets of A4 paper. Very thin plastic bag material, sellotape, cottton, clothes peg.

Experiment 1: Aim - to help children understand that the shape of an object can effect how quickly the object falls to the ground.

It is important for the children to realise that for a fair test the two objects should be released at the same time.

The point to be drawn out is that the resistance of the air slows the descent of the larger, flatter shaped objects.

Experiment 2: Aim - to help the children to construct a working model parachute, thus incorporating the learning experiences from experiment 1.

It is important to have very thin, light plastic material, cut approximately into a 30/40 cm square. Use only a small amount of sellotape to attach cotton thread to each of the four corners. Experiment with different types of plastic pegs/toy men for best performance. This is best tried by the teacher before introducing the experiment to the children.

Questions to answer

The point to be drawn out is that the space shuttle was developed to replace early space craft which could only be used once.

Problems to solve

These extension activities are for those children who would like to improve their parachute design, by further experimentation.

Experiment 1 - How quickly do things drop?

Take two sheets of paper the same size and screw one into a ball. Stand on a chair and let them go at the same time. Which hits the ground first? Why? Try different shaped pieces of paper.

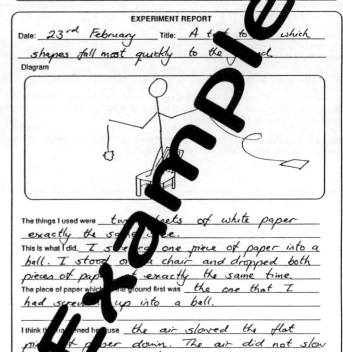

Experiment 2 - Can you make a toy parachute?

Cut a large square of very thin 'plastic bag material', sellotape a length of cotton to each corner and tie the ends to a clothes peg. Throw it into the air and observe what happens. Improve your design.

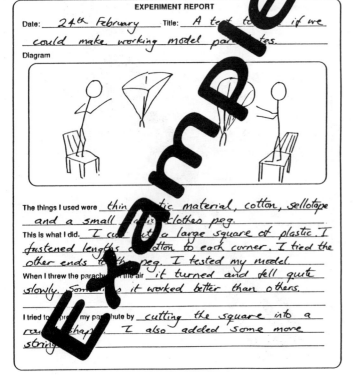

Questions to answer

1) What is special about the Space Shuttle? _The Space Shuttle is special because it can be used again._
2) How did the spacecraft land before the shuttle? _Spacecraft landed before the shuttle, by using parachutes._
3) What used to be left in space? _Most of the rocket used to be left in space._
4) Who travelled inside the space capsule? _The astronauts travelled inside the space capsule._
5) Why did one sheet of paper fall slowly? _One sheet of paper fell slowly because it acted as a parachute._
6) How does the space shuttle return to earth? _The space shuttle glides back to earth like a plane._

Problems to solve

Can you improve your parachute by changing its shape, the number of strings, the weight it carries etc?

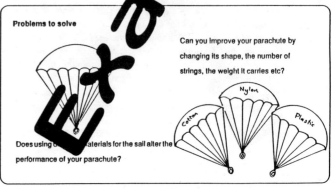

Does using other materials for the sail alter the performance of your parachute?

Level 3 - HOW CAN MESSAGES BE SENT? - Teacher's Notes

Equipment needed: 2 washing-up liquid bottles, a sharp knife (for teacher use), one metre of narrow P.V.C. tubing (available from a wine-making shop), two small empty baked beans cans, with all jagged edges removed from one end and a small hole pierced in the centre of the complete end, some string and a pair of scissors.

Experiment 1: Aim - to help children understand that sound can be made to travel through a medium such as P.V.C. tubing.

Cut the washing-up liquid bottles in half and attach the P.V.C. tubing as shown in the diagram.

The children should be able to use this device as a very simple telephone.

Experiment 2: Aim - to help the children understand that sound can be passed some distance along a taut string.

The two tins are connected by 3/4m of string, as shown in the diagram.

The point to be drawn out is the telephone will only work when the string is taut.

Questions to answer

The point should be drawn out that, due to the invention of radio and television, telephone links no longer need to be physically joined together.

Problems to solve

This extension activity is for those children who would like to improve the design of their telephone through further experimentation.

Experiment 1 - Can you make a washing-up liquid bottle telephone?

Find two washing-up liquid bottles which have been cut in half. Connect some plastic tubing to the nozzles. Can this be used as a simple telephone? Will it work round corners?

EXPERIMENT REPORT

Date: 16th March   Title: A test to see if a telephone can be made from plastic bottles.

Diagram

The things I used were two washing-up liquid bottles and some plastic tubing.
This is what I did. I pushed the tubing onto the nozzles of the plastic bottles. I spoke into one end. My friend listened at the other. We tried it round a corner.
When I spoke into the washing-up liquid bottle my friend could hear what I was saying. The sound seemed to go along the tube.
When we used the 'telephone' round a corner it did not work very well. It seemed to work best when the tube was straight.

Experiment 2 - Can you send sound along a string?

Find or make a string telephone using two tins and a piece of string. Pull the string tight and try to speak to your partner. What happens? Will it work if the string is slack? Will it work round corners?

EXPERIMENT REPORT

Date: 17th March   Title: A test to see if sound can be sent along a string.

Diagram

The things I used were two tins and a long piece of string.
This is what I did. We pushed the string through holes in the tins and tied knots. We pulled the string tight. I spoke in one end and my friend could hear me.
When I tried to speak to my partner she could hear what I was saying.
When the line was slack the tin telephone would not work.
We tried round a corner and the telephone worked a little but not very well.

Questions to answer

1) How do astronauts speak to earth? Astronauts speak to earth by using T.V. or radio.
2) What does the camera in the space-craft do? The camera in the spacecraft takes the pictures.
3) What does the transmitter do? The transmitter sends electrical signals to earth.
4) What does the receiving aerial do? The receiving aerial collects the signals and sends them to a television.
5) Is the spacecraft connected to base control by wires? The spacecraft is not connected to earth with wires.
6) Why do you think it is important to have a tight string on your telephone? It is important to have a tight string on a toy telephone so the sound can vibrate along the string.

Problems to solve

What is the greatest distance your string telephone will work over? Can you improve the design? Can you make a speaking <u>and</u> a listening part?

Research other ways of sending messages.
How did the Romans send messages?

Level 3 - DOES THE MOON CHANGE SHAPE? - Teacher's Notes

Equipment needed: A desk lamp or table lamp with the shade removed and a white table-tennis ball.

Experiment 1: Aim - to help children understand why it is impossible for us to view the dark side of the moon from the Earth.

This experiment is best carried out in an open space i.e. large hall or playground. One pupil is asked to walk around another without allowing the stationary pupil to see his/her back. This is easily achieved by stepping side-ways.

The point to be drawn out is that it is impossible to observe the dark side of the moon from the earth because the moon, like the person stepping sideways, always displays the same face.

Experiment 2: Aim - to help the children understand that the apparent change in shape of the moon is caused by its position in orbit around the Earth, relative to the sun.

This experiment is best carried out in a darkened room. The movement of the white ball around the stationary observer produces shadow shapes similar to those which cause the different phases of the moon.

The point to be drawn out is that different moon shapes observed are caused by only part of the moon being illuminated at different stages in the month.

Questions to answer

The children should realise that the Moon is the Earth's only natural satellite and can only be seen so clearly because it is the closest object to us in space.

Problems to solve

These extension activities are for those pupils who are interested in making regular moon observations during darkness.

Experiment 1 - Why can you not see the back of the Moon?

Choose one person to be the 'earth' and another to be the 'moon'. Ask the 'moon' to walk round the earth in a circle without showing his back - the earth turning on the spot to face the moon. Can it be done?

EXPERIMENT REPORT

Date: 25/11/91 Title: An experiment to investigate why we cannot see the far side of the moon.

Diagram

Equipment needed: two people and a large space to work in.

Method used: I stood in the centre of the room. My friend walked sideways in a large circle around me. I watched my friend by turning on the spot.

Observations made: Even though I kept looking at my friend, he managed to walk right round me without ever showing his back to me.

Why do you think we cannot see the back of the Moon from the Earth's surface? I think we cannot see the back of the moon because the moon always keeps the same side looking towards the earth.

Experiment 2 - Does the Moon change shape?

Use a lamp to represent the sun and a small white ball to represent the Moon in a darkened room. Stand about 1 m from the lamp. (You represent the earth). Move the white ball round your head. What shadow shapes do you observe on the white ball?

EXPERIMENT REPORT

Date: 26/11/91 Title: An experiment to investigate how the moon appears to change its shape.

Diagram

Equipment needed: a desk lamp, a small white ball and a darkened room.

Method used: I stood in front of a lighted desk lamp in a darkened room. I moved the white ball round my head and looked at the shadow shapes formed on the ball.

Observations made: The white ball went from being completely lit up, to half lit up, to completely in shadow.

Why do you think the moon appears to change shape week by week? I think the moon appears to change shape because of its position in orbit around the earth and hence how much of it's surface is lit up by the sun.

Questions to answer

1) Why does the moon look so large in the night sky? The moon looks large because it is relatively close to the earth.

2) Is the moon larger than the sun? The moon is much smaller than the sun.

3) What is an unnatural satellite? An unnatural satellite is a man-made object orbiting a planet.

4) How many people do you think you could lift if you were standing on the moon? I think I could lift six people on the moon.

5) What makes the moon 'light up'? The moon is lit up when it reflects light from the sun.

6) Does the moon change its shape? The moon does not really change shape. The thing that changes is the shape of the reflected light.

Problems to solve

Can you make accurate observations of the Moon's surface using binoculars or a telescope?

Devise and carry out a way of recording Moon observations over a period of one month.

Level 4 - WHY DO WE HAVE DAY AND NIGHT? - Teacher's Notes

Equipment needed: shoe box and lid, a torch, a matchbox sized toy car, a globe, blu-tack.

Experiment 1: Aim - to help children understand that without a source of light, objects are naturally in darkness.

The cardboard box needs a small peep-hole (approx size of a 2p coin) cut in one end and a circular hole cut into the lid the same size as the torch face. It is important to let as little natural light through this point as possible.

The point to be drawn out is that when we have a source of light, objects can be clearly seen, as in daylight hours. Without a source of light darkness prevails.

Experiment 2: Aim - to help children understand that our day and night are created by the earth revolving in front of a source of light.

This experiment will work best in a darkened room. A piece of blu-tack can be used to mark Great Britain. The light source must remain static. As the globe is revolved anti-clockwise the blu-tack will move from light into dark.

The point to be drawn out is that day and night are caused by the earth revolving in front of its light source - the sun.

Questions to answer

The questions about morning and night refer to daytime and night-time activities.

Problems to solve

Various means could be devised for dimming the light including a 'sliding card cover' over the opening.

Light shone on the globe can be varied by raising or lowering the light source.

Experiment 1 - How can you make light and dark?

Find a closed box with a small hole to peep through and a larger hole for a torch. Put a toy car inside the box. Now start your report.

Date: Wednesday 3rd November.
Title: Making things light and dark.
Picture of what you did.

I needed an old shoe box with two holes cut in it, a torch and a toy car.
I peeped inside with the torch switched on and I could see the toy car clearly inside the box.
With the torch switched off I could see darkness. It was almost impossible to see the toy car.
To make daylight inside the box I needed a torch to light up the inside of the box. If I took the lid off this made it light inside the box as well.

Experiment 2 - How can you make day and night?

Find a globe and a torch. Shine the torch onto the globe. (The torch is like the sun. The globe is like the earth). Put a small piece of blu-tack on England. Turn the globe slowly anticlockwise. Start your report.

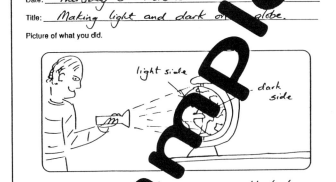

Date: Thursday 5th November
Title: Making light and dark on a globe.
Picture of what you did.

I needed a torch, a globe and some blu-tack.
I shone the torch onto the globe and only one side of it was lit up.
England was in day light when it was on the side lit up by the torch.
England was in darkness when it was on the side away from the torch light.
The globe turning round in front of a light and then away from the light makes us have daylight and then darkness. We call this night and day.

Questions to answer

1) What do we do in the morning? In the morning we get up, get dressed and have our breakfast.
2) What do we do at night time? At night time we put our pyjamas on, brush our teeth and go to bed.
3) When do we get our longest days? We get our longest days in the summer time.
4) When do we get our longest nights? We get our longest nights in the middle of the winter.
5) What do we need for day light? To have day light we need the sun shining on our side of the earth.
6) Why do we have day and night? We have night and day because the earth turns in front of our giant light, the sun.

Problems to solve

Can you make the light in the box turn to darkness gradually?

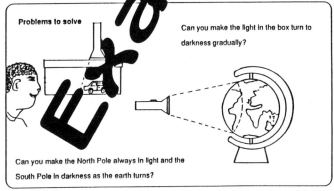

Can you make the North Pole always in light and the South Pole in darkness as the earth turns?

Level 4 - HOW DO ASTRONAUTS STAY ALIVE IN SPACE? - Teacher's Notes

Equipment needed: two empty 'coke type' tins, a small empty cardboard box with a lid, a thermometer marked in degrees centigrade, some newspaper, a source of hot water and a margarine tub.

Experiment 1: Aim - to help children understand that by insulating water containers, the contents can be kept at a higher temperature for a longer period of time than without insulation.

The torn up scraps of newspaper packed lightly around one container standing inside a cardboard box acts as insulation. The experiment will work best if very hot (not necessarily boiling) water can be used. Care must always be taken when young children are using hot water.

The point should be made that this is a simple example of energy conservation.

Experiment 2: Aim - to help the children understand how a simple cooling system operates. Again the two tins should be filled with hot water, but this time, one tin is placed inside a 2 litre ice-cream/margarine container. The container is then placed under a slow running cold tap. (see diagram)

The container is allowed to fill with cold water and overflow. The movement of the cold water around the tin creates a simple cooling system which causes the water inside the tin to cool rapidly.

The point should be made that this is one way of keeping things cool.

Questions to answer

It should be drawn out that space suits have a number of different functions to perform, including supplying oxygen, providing insulation and providing a cooling system when necessary.

Problems to solve

These extension activities are designed for pupils who wish to investigate insulation and cooling systems further.

NOTE: The second activity involves the use of boiling water. This should only be allowed under careful adult supervision.

Experiment 1 - How can we keep things warm?

You will need two empty 'coke' tins, a cardboard box with a lid, a thermometer, some torn up newspaper and some very hot water. Put one tin in the box and pack round with newspaper scraps. Fill the tins with hot water. Use a thermometer to measure how hot the water is every five minutes.

EXPERIMENT REPORT

Date: 23/9/90 Title: An experiment to investigate how to keep things warm

Diagram

Equipment needed: two 'coke type' tins, a cardboard box, a thermometer, scraps of paper and hot water.
Method used: One tin was packed in a box with paper scraps. Both tins were filled with hot water. The temperature of the water was measured every 5 minutes.

Observations made:

TIME	Temperature of tin in air	Temperature of tin in box
0 minutes	50 °C	50 °C
5 minutes	45 °C	50 °C
10 minutes	40 °C	48 °C
15 minutes	38 °C	47 °C
20 minutes	37 °C	45 °C
25 minutes	35 °C	44 °C
30 minutes	34 °C	43 °C

Which tin stayed warm the longer? Why? The tin in the box stayed warm the longer. The packing kept the heat in.

Experiment 2 - How can we keep things cool?

You will need two empty 'coke' tins, thermometer and a plastic margarine tub. Fill the tins with hot water. Put one tin into the margarine tub. Place the margarine tub under a running cold tap. Use a thermometer to measure how hot the water is in each can, every five minutes.

EXPERIMENT REPORT

Date: 24/9/90 Title: An experiment to investigate how to cool things down

Diagram

Equipment needed: two 'coke type' tins, a plastic margarine tub, a thermometer, hot water and cold running water.
Method used: Both tins were filled with hot water. One tin was stood in a tub of cold water under a running tap. The temperature of the water was measured every 5 minutes.

Observations made:

TIME	Temperature of tin in air	Temperature of tin in box
0 minutes	58 °C	58 °C
5 minutes	55 °C	32 °C
10 minutes	43 °C	25 °C
15 minutes	40 °C	20 °C
20 minutes	38 °C	18 °C
25 minutes	37 °C	17 °C
30 minutes	36 °C	17 °C

Which tin cooled more quickly? The tin in the cold water cooled more quickly. The moving cold water took the heat away.

Questions to answer

1) Why do you think astronauts don't need to wear their space suits inside the space craft? Astronauts don't wear their suits inside because the spacecraft provides oxygen and a constant temperature.

2) Why do the suits have air tanks? Space suits need air tanks because there is no air to breathe in space.

3) How could a space suit be made to cool an astronaut down? A space suit could have a built in cooling system.

4) What could be done to make sure a space suit stays nice and warm? A space suit could be well insulated.

5) Why is the astronaut fastened to the spacecraft by a cable? An astronaut may use a cable to stop himself floating away.

6) Do you think a space suit would be comfortable to wear? Why? I think a space suit would be uncomfortable because it would be very bulky.

Problems to solve

How good are other materials at keeping water warm?

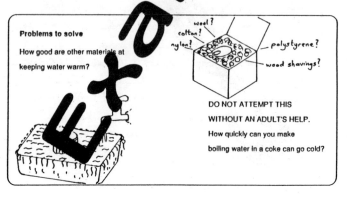

DO NOT ATTEMPT THIS WITHOUT AN ADULT'S HELP.

How quickly can you make boiling water in a coke can go cold?

Level 4 - WHAT IS GRAVITY? - Teacher's Notes

Equipment needed: a selection of stones of different sizes, 2 washing-up liquid bottles and some nylon line.
A washing-up liquid aeroplane needs to be constructed by the teacher as shown in the diagram. One washing-up liquid bottle should be cut to make a simple aeroplane body shape. The second washing-up liquid bottle has the top 10cm sliced away from the lower part which is discarded. This funnel shape is fitted into the rear part of the body of the model plane. This provides a route through which the nylon line can be fed. An old ruler can be used to make the wings and tail fins can be made from card.

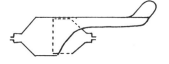

Experiment 1: Aim - to help children understand that the weight of an object does not effect how quickly it falls to the earth. It is important that the children realise that the stones should travel the same distance and be released at exactly the same time, for a fair test to be made.

Experiment 2: Aim - to help the children understand that gravity can pull objects to earth, even at an angle. The children should experiment with sliding the model plane down the nylon line held at various angles. It should become apparent that the steeper the slope, the more quickly the plane travels.

The point to be drawn out is that it is gravity acting on the model plane that causes it to move.

Questions to answer

Children should realise that gravity is an invisible force which works on all objects. However, the point should be made that in Earth orbit, gravity has no effect

Problems to solve

These extension activities provide opportunities for design technology work.

Experiment 1 - Do heavy objects fall more quickly?

Hold a stone in your hand. Let it go. What happens? Hold a large stone and a small stone at the same height. Let them go at exactly the same time. Which landed first? Was your test fair?

EXPERIMENT REPORT

Date: 14/10/90   Title: An experiment to investigate falling stones.

Diagram

Equipment needed: a selection of different sized stones and a high place to drop them.

Method used: I dropped a stone and watched it fall. I dropped different sized stones at the same time and watched them fall.

Observations made: The stones always fell straight down. When dropped at the same time the stones always landed at exactly the same time.

Do heavy stones fall more quickly than light ones? The heavy stones appeared to fall at the same speed as the lighter stones.

Experiment 2 - Does gravity work on a slope?

Ask your teacher for a washing-up liquid aeroplane. Thread some nylon line through the nozzles of the plane. Hold one end of the line high and one end low. Let go of the plane. What happens? When does it move most quickly?

EXPERIMENT REPORT

Date: 15/10/90   Title: An experiment to investigate the performance of a sliding line model plane

Diagram

Equipment needed: a sliding line model plane made from two washing-up liquid bottles and a length of nylon line.

Method used: The line was threaded through the plane. The plane was held high and released to slide down the nylon line slope.

Observations made: The steeper the slope of the nylon line the quicker the model plane moved down.

What made the plane move along the line? The earth's invisible force called gravity pulled the plane down the nylon line.

Questions to answer

1) What makes an apple fall out of a tree? Gravity makes an apple fall out of a tree when the fruit is ripe.

2) What do magnets attract? Magnets attract some other objects and other magnets.

3) What does gravity attract? Gravity attracts everything.

4) What happens to astronauts in space? Astronauts become weightless in space and float around.

5) Which way did the stones always fall? Why? The stones always fell downwards because gravity attracted them.

6) What made the model plane slide down the string? Gravity was the invisible force pulling the model plane down the string.

Problems to solve

Can you make a machine that will drop two different stones at exactly the same time?

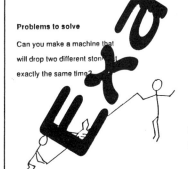

Can you make a nylon line plane which will travel faster than any other?

Level 4 - WHY ARE SUMMER DAYS LONGER THAN WINTER DAYS? - Teacher's Notes

Equipment needed: A table lamp without a shade, a white tennis-size ball marked as in the diagram.
A knitting needle should be pushed through the ball from North to South.
A torch and a flat piece of centimetre squared paper.

Experiment 1: Aim - to help children understand that the tilt of the Earth's axis and the journey the Earth makes around the sun are together responsible for the length of the daylight hours.

This experiment is best carried out in a darkened room. By holding the ball (the Earth) at a fixed angle and moving it round the table lamp (the sun) it can be seen that there are times when the Northern hemisphere receives more light than the Southern hemisphere. If the ball (the Earth) is rotated on its own axis (the knitting needle), as it makes this journey around the sun, it can be seen that at one end of the sun orbit the Northern hemisphere will have a longer day than at the opposite end of the sun orbit.

The point to be drawn out is that it is a combination of the Earth's tilt and its journey around the sun that causes longer and shorter days.

Experiment 2: Aim - to help the children understand that it is the intensity of the suns rays, which cause higher temperatures in summer months and lower temperatures in winter months.

This experiment is best carried out in a darkened room. The children will discover that the beam from the torch held at an angle covers a greater area.

The point to be drawn out is that the torch (the sun) always emits the same amount of light. If it shines directly down, the light is more intense than when it shines from an angle and is spread over a greater area. This principle is exactly the same in the case of the sun's heat radiation directed towards the Earth. In summer, the Earth's axis is tilted towards the Sun and the heat radiation focuses on a relatively small area. In winter, the Earth's axis is tilted away from the sun and the same amount of heat focuses on a larger area.

Questions to answer

The children should realise that seasonal changes are brought about by the change in the length of day and changes in the temperature of the Earth.

Problems to solve

These extension activities are for those children who wish to investigate further the temperatures experienced by the British Isles.

This is an example page from a teacher's resource showing completed experiment reports on the topic of why summer days are longer than winter days, including Experiment 1 (using a lamp and ball to model Earth's orbit) and Experiment 2 (using a torch and squared paper to show light intensity at different angles).

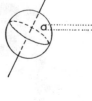

Research the seasons experienced by the North Pole and the Equator.

Level 5 - WHAT IS A STAR? - Teacher's Notes

Equipment needed: 2 cardboard tubes approx. 20cm long (one tube should fit inside the other), a hand lens with a focal length of 30 cm and another with a focal length of 2 - 3 cm, blu-tack, a one metre diameter circle of black sugar paper and drawing pins.

Experiment 1: Aim - to help the children understand that far away objects can be made to appear to look closer using a system of lenses.

The exact focal lengths of the lenses is not critical, trial and error will soon reveal if the lenses available will act like a telescope. For the best effects, the lenses should be fastened into the ends of the tube using blu-tack to secure and black out external light. One tube should be a neat fit inside the other.
The point to be drawn out is that, although the objects look closer, they have not moved.

Experiment 2: Aim - to help the children understand that the movement of star patterns observed in the night sky are in fact due to the rotation of the earth.

Much discussion will need to acompany this activity. The children are asked to observe a stationary pattern, which will appear to move as they make their observations whilst moving round the perimeter of the classroom. The teacher should attempt to link this to night time observations made from a rotating planet.

Questions to answer

The point should be made that our sun is a star, the same as any other found in the night sky.

Problems to solve

This extension activity will help the children to understand the cycle of change the moon goes through in one month.

Experiment 1 - Can you make a working model telescope?

You need two tubes about 20cm long. One tube should fit inside the other. You also need blu-tack and two lenses (ask your teacher). Use blu-tack to fit a lens into one end of each tube. Fit the tubes together. Use your telescope to make observations in and around your classroom.
* NEVER LOOK DIRECTLY AT THE SUN*

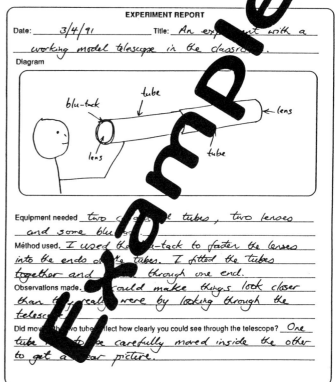

Experiment 2 - Do stars move across our night sky?

Copy the front page diagram onto a 1m circle of sugar paper. Pin this to the ceiling in the centre of your classrooom. Stand in a corner of the room and with your telescope observe the star patterns. Keeping watch, walk slowly anti-clockwise round the classroom. What do you notice?

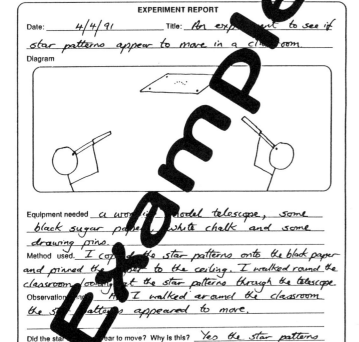

Questions to answer

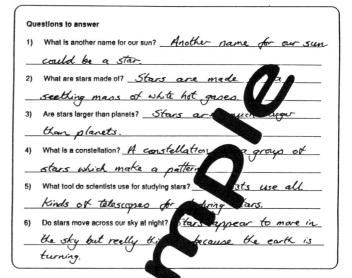

Problems to solve

Research some names of constellations. Where did these names come from?

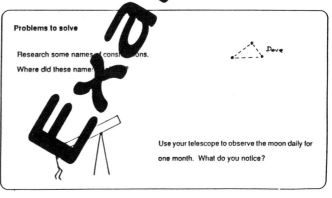

Use your telescope to observe the moon daily for one month. What do you notice?

Level 5 - WHAT IS THE SOLAR SYSTEM? - Teacher's Notes

Equipment needed: nine planet names written on card, 4 P.E. hoops approximately 1 metre in diameter, paper, glue, yellow tissue paper, plasticine and thin thread.

Experiment 1: Aim - to help children understand that the greater the distance from the centre of a circle, the longer it takes to travel around the circumference (if speed is constant).

The nine pupils should stand in a straight line from the chair with the pupil holding the Mercury card closest to the chair. They are asked to walk in a circle in the same direction. To do this accurately, it may be necessary to chalk out the appropriate routes, on the ground.

The point to be drawn out is that the "planet" furthest from the sun takes the longest time to make one complete orbit.

How to make a model solar system

Following the instructions on the pupil activity sheet, a model solar system can be constructed in the classroom. It is important to realise that the planets are in correct proportion to the size of the sun, but the distances between the planets are not. For a more realistic model using sun and planets of these dimensions, a large open space is needed as detailed in "Problems to solve".

Questions to answer

The point to be drawn out is that our solar system is made up of the sun, and the nine planets which orbit it.

Problems to solve

The first activity helps to create a more realistic model of the Solar System. Secondary sources can be used to research the asteroid belt.

Experiment 1 - Which planet takes the longest to orbit the sun?

You need 9 planet name cards and a chair. Place the chair in the middle of your playground (this represents the sun). Ask 9 pupils to hold a card and stand in planet order from the chair (sun). Walking at the same speed, ask the pupils to walk in a circle round the chair. Which pupil takes the longest?

EXPERIMENT REPORT

Date: 19/6/91 Title: An experiment to investigate how quickly planets go round the sun.

Diagram

Equipment needed: nine pieces of card with planet names written on them and a chair.

Method used: We placed a chair in the playground. Nine children stood in a line from the chair holding planet name cards. The children walked round the chair in a circle.

Observations made: The children at the end of the line took much longer to walk around the chair than the child who was nearest to the chair.

Which planet do you think would take the longest to orbit the sun? I think the planet Pluto would take longest to orbit the sun because of the distance it has to travel.

HOW TO MAKE A MODEL SOLAR SYSTEM

1) Use P.E. hoops to make a 1 metre diameter globe framework. Cover the frame with strips of thick paper and then papier-mache. Finally cover with yellow tissue paper. This represents the sun.

2) Make 9 planets from plasticine balls to these sizes:

   Mercury 1/2 cm across
   Venus 1 cm across
   Earth 1 cm across
   Mars 1/2 cm across
   Jupiter 11 cm across
   Saturn 9 1/2 cm across
   Uranus 4 cm across
   Neptune 4 cm across
   Pluto 1/4 cm across

   Cover the balls with papier-mache. Research planet colours and paint the models appropriately. Make Saturn and Uranus cardboard rings.

3) Hang the 'sun' in one corner of the classroom from the ceiling. Working diagonally across the room, use thread to suspend the planets the following distances from the sun.

   Mercury 10 cm, Venus 20 cm, Earth 30 cm, Mars 40 cm, Jupiter 150 cm, Saturn 280 cm, Uranus 580 cm, Neptune 900 cm, Pluto 1200 cm.*

Questions to answer

1) What is the Solar System? The Solar System is everything which moves around our sun.

2) What is a Satellite? A Satellite is anything which moves around a planet.

3) What is the nearest planet to the sun? The nearest planet to our sun is Mercury.

4) Which planet is furthest from the sun? The planet which is furthest from our sun is Pluto.

5) Which planet orbits the sun in the shortest time? Mercury orbits the sun in the shortest time.

6) Why is this? Mercury orbits in the shortest time because it travels the shortest distance of all the planets.

Problems to solve

Space distances are enormous. For a more accurate model, multiply all distances from the sun by 400. Will the model fit your school field?

What is the asteroid belt?

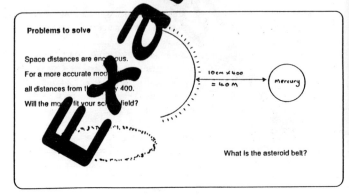